Introduction

If you are a first-time buyer, or even if you are looking to buy your second or third slice of real estate, it can often seem overwhelming when you are viewing residential homes.

Whilst it is obviously very exciting to look at homes, and picture yourself living there or indeed what may be possible to change, it is natural to be concerned that you are not asking the right questions or are missing something important.

Obviously, after making an offer to buy, many people will employ a surveyor to find out whether there are any building defects for piece of mind. But employing a surveyor is not free of charge and, once the offer is made, it is sometimes difficult to renegotiate the offer price based on survey findings.

It is also important that you educate yourself on the basic construction of a house, at least to be able to understand a building report, particularly because buying a home is the largest single purchase most people will ever make.

The purpose of this guide is to prepare you for looking at real estate. What are the main considerations which you should think about, and how to quickly identify some of the most common building defects.

Armed with the knowledge from this guide, you should be able to identify all of the most common defects upon first inspection of the piece of real estate, meaning that you will not waste your time or energy in starting the buying process on a home which contains defects which are too much for either your stress levels or your purse… or both!

Also, knowing the defects upon first inspection will enable you to roughly calculate the remediation costs, in order that you can make your offer on a well-informed basis. There is no doubt that this knowledge could save you a ton of cash.

It also goes to say that very few houses or apartments you view will be absolutely perfect, even if it is new-build. You should always expect to find a couple defects no matter how stunning the place is. But the identification and cost of rectifying those defects could either help you negotiate the best deal, or could provide you with enough information to make you walk away.

There are eight key categories which you should look out for; Structure, Damp, Rot, Security, Utilities, Roof, Outside, and Miscellaneous.

Obviously, depending on the type of real estate which you are looking to purchase (such as a studio apartment versus a family house), some of these categories might not be applicable. But it's always useful to bear all of this in mind.

Structure

The overall structure of the building is one of the most visibly obvious signs of major defects, and can be seen by the conditions of the walls.

It is important to understand that buildings always slightly move, for example due to annual changes in weather climate or the gradual settling of the ground beneath. This is completely normal.

To identify if there are any issues with the structure, you look for any cracks in any of the walls both on the inside and the outside. If you see "hairline" cracks, these are cracks which are barely visible and about the width of a hair, this is completely normal. These can often be easily fixed with just a layer of paint or wallpaper, or indeed a thin smear of wall filler.

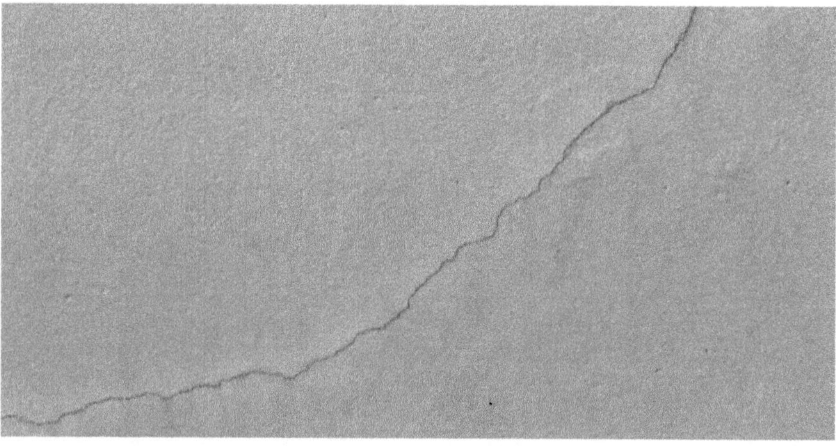

(example of a hairline crack)

However, if you can comfortably fit a credit card or even your fingers into the crack, it could indicate a more serious problem and you should always consider getting it checked. When looking for wall cracks, you should pay special attention around the windows and doors, because these are usually the weak points of any wall.

(example of a problem crack)

If the building has been extended, you should pay special attention to where the extension fits the main building. You should look for any cracks both inside and outside.

If the building has any exposed stonework or brickwork, you also need to take a look at the pointing, which is the cement between the stones or bricks. You are looking to check that it is in good solid condition, and whether there are any gaps or holes which are not part of the design. Any gaps or holes could cause water ingress when raining, potentially causing structural and damp issues.

(example of a brick wall which requires attention)

Whilst looking at the walls, you should also take a quick look down the line of each wall. If the building has been built during the past 200-300 years, none of the walls should lean or bulge. Also, check that the chimney is straight and is truly vertical. If any of these features are not completely straight, it could indicate that the building is not structurally sound, and you should always seek specialist advice.

(example of a bulging wall, note the horizontal cracking)

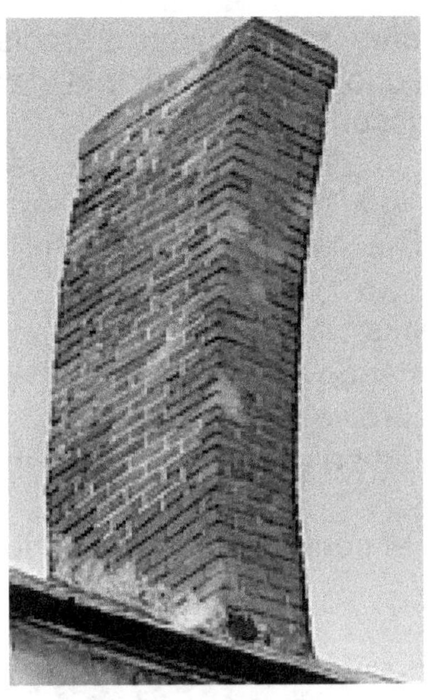

(example of a leaning chimney, requiring attention)

Damp

Small signs of damp is not always a problem, but when damp is sustained for a long time, that's when problems can very easily occur!

The first thing to look for is any visible signs of dampness in every room. This can be any of the following:

- Water marks
- Peeling or soggy wallpaper
- Yellow or brown staining on walls
- Black mould patches, particularly in the corners of the room
- Evidence of condensation on windows

(example of peeling wallpaper due to dampness)

(example of damp staining on walls)

(example of damp staining behind curtains)

The key places to check are the corners of the room, just above the skirting boards (otherwise known as base boards), and the corners of the ceilings. Pay special attention around window and door frames, and don't be afraid to look behind the curtains or any furniture for such warning signs.

You should also pay special attention to bathrooms and shower rooms, because these rooms require a lot of ventilation to avoid any prolonged dampness. In most countries, it is mandatory to have mechanical ventilation fans to help expel any damp air, so it is worth making sure that such fans are working. Bathrooms are particularly vulnerable to black mould, which grows due to prolonged dampness.

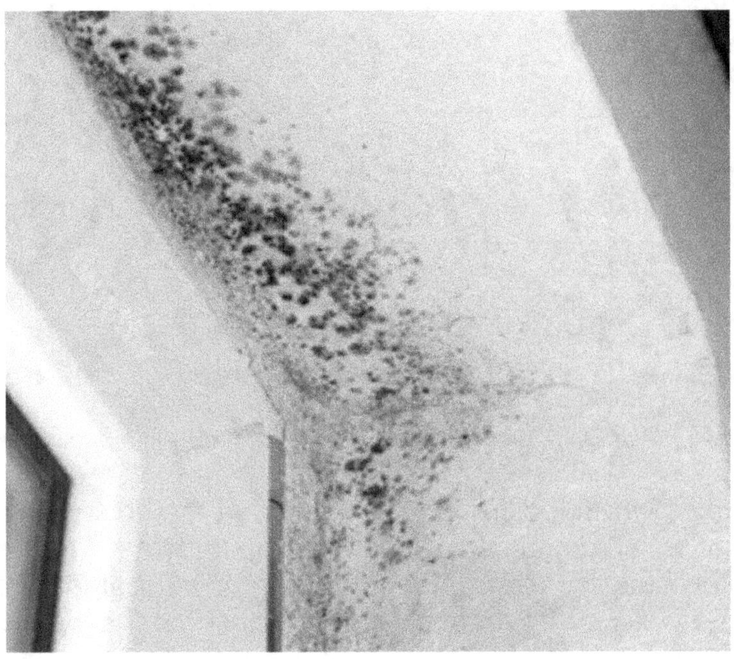

(example of black mould around a bathroom window)

Black mould can often be easily remedied by the improvement of ventilation before cleaning and redecorating affected areas. However, sometimes, the mould could indicate underlying dampness issues on the surface with other causes.

You may see also black mould on the grout (between ceramic tiles) or the silicone sealing around sinks, showers and baths. However, this is very normal, and can be easily removed by either using household bleach, or by raking out and applying new silicone.

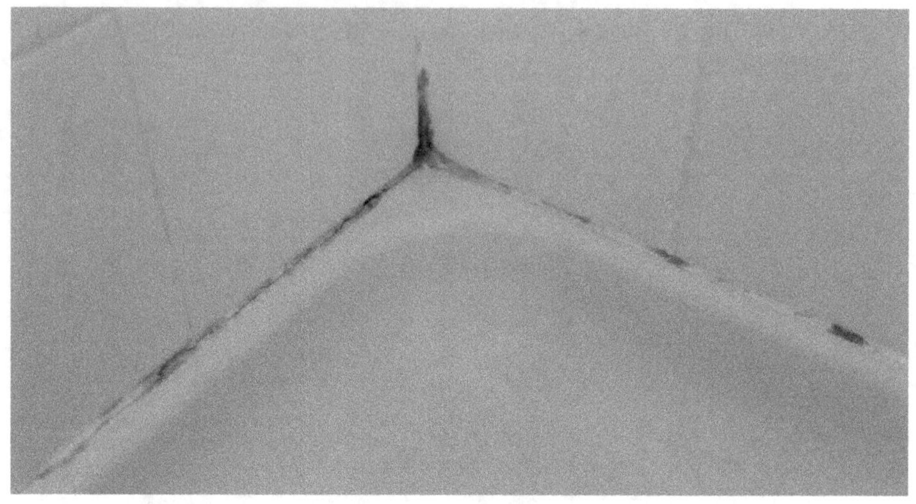

(example of black mould in the silicone seal around a shower tray)

It is also worth looking on the outside of the house for any stains which could be caused by dripping water (from a broken gutter for example). Look for moss or algae growth on the walls, or any other warning signs that the walls have been exposed to prolonged dampness.

Rot

Looking for rot is often one of the easiest things to overlook when you view a house, but is also something which could cost a very large amount to put right!

Check any places where there is wood - window and door frames, door steps, window sills, skirting boards or base boards, and any original wood floors.

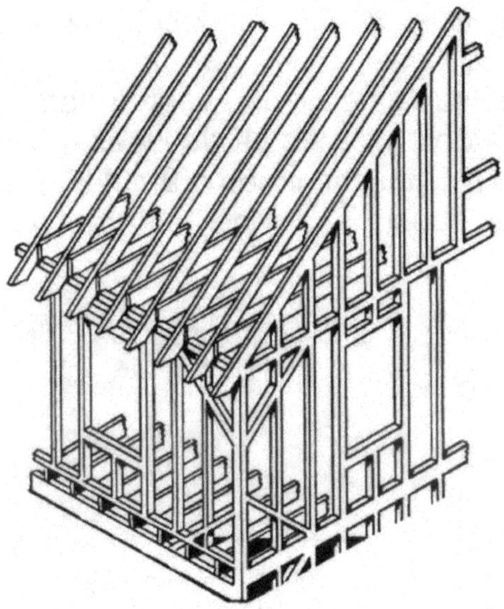

What you are looking for on any naked or varnished wood is any signs of dark discolouration, chunks missing, evidence of fungus, and indeed any evidence of filler being recently applied. You also need to check any painted wood, specifically for any bubbling or uneven areas on the paint, usually near the end or where the wood joins another piece.

(example of dry rot on the end of a wood plank)

If you find any such areas, use your fingernail or take a key and give the wood a gentle prod. Does the key easily sink into the wood? Does the wood crumble? If so, you should definitely seek specialist advice as part of your negotiation.

(example of rot underneath painted wood)

Another useful trick is that, if you know the floor joists are made of wood, go to the middle of the room and gently jump. This might look strange, but what you are looking for is whether the floor feels solid or springy? If a floor with wood joists feels springy, it is highly likely to contain rot.

If you find rot in several places in your investigation, it is possible that it could have penetrated the entire home. Some types of rot are actually species of fungus and, once the spores are in the air, it can be very unhealthy for the inhabitants and can also cause the problem to spread quickly. If the building is found to have significant rot throughout, it will have to be professionally sprayed to kill the spores, along with the cutting-out and replacement of wood. A house with wood rot can potentially cost a very large amount of money to put right!

Security

Depending on the location of the building, security could be a key feature to look at, particularly in busy towns or cities.

You should check if there is a functioning burglar alarm and fire alarm system. Also, check if there are any wired smoke detectors, and indeed carbon monoxide detectors if there is gas connected to the building.

Are there security lights installed? Is there a video doorbell?

Do all the windows have adequate locks? And do the doors have locks that would meet with insurer standards?

Now, many of these items can be rectified fairly cheaply, but you need to bear these costs in mind when making your offer!

Utilities

When considering utilities, the main expense here is usually the boiler system, so you should always check the boiler type and when it last serviced.

Also, if there is a water tank for the hot water system, you should also check the type and the last service date.

(example of a hot water cylinder)

The next thing to take a look at is the electricity cupboard. What you are looking for is the style and condition of the power sockets, light switches, and so on. How old are the components and wiring likely to be? And always ask when the last safety check was, if this is not recorded on or near the fuse box.

If there are any gas appliances, you should always find out when the last check was performed. When either electricity or gas is concerned, you certainly don't want to take any risks, as these are both potentially fire hazards!

If there is heating, what type is it? If there are radiators, are they all in good condition? Do they have individual thermostats? Are the sizes of the radiators appropriate for the room?

(example of a water-filled radiator)

If there is any underfloor heating, always take a look at where the control pipes are located and look for any obvious signs of leakage. Also, how old is the water pump?

(example of a typical underfloor heating setup, the pump is the unit on the right)

If there is air conditioning, how old is the unit and when was it last serviced?

Finally, check the water system. Briefly turn the taps on and listen for any knocking sounds from the plumbing, which could indicate pipes being secured incorrectly. Check that the water drains correctly and does not collect in the shower, bath or basin. And also check that the toilets flush correctly.

Roof

The roof is one of the most visible and important elements of any building, keeping the rain and dampness outside.

If you can get access to the roof from the inside, you should always take a look up there. The first thing to check is whether the attic is insulated. A well-insulated attic will help maintain a cooler home in the warmer months, a warmer home in the winter months, and will certainly help with energy efficiencies.

(example of an insulated attic, "cold roof" style)

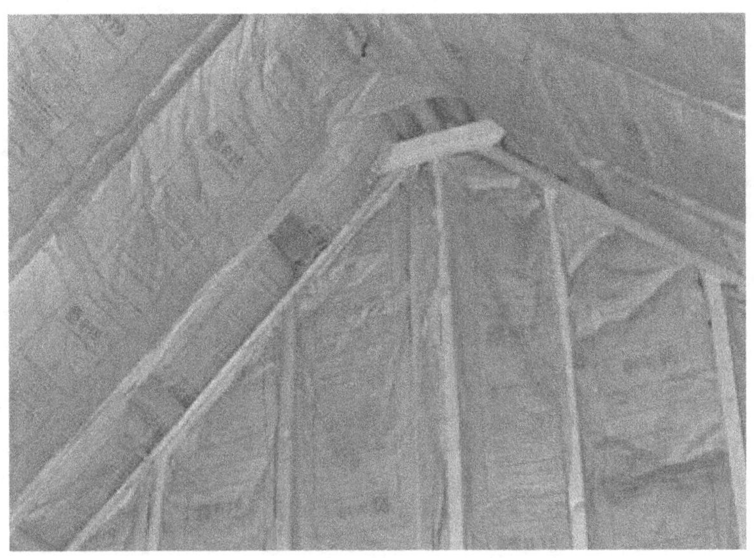

(example of an insulated attic, "warm roof" style)

The next thing to look at is whether there is any evidence of whether water can penetrate. Can you see any light shining through any gaps in the roof, or can you see any water stains on the structure?

Whilst looking at the roof structure, always check for any signs of rot also. Although Rot was covered in an earlier section, it is of note that many types of rot tend to start in the roof, as this is usually one of the places which can easily get damp.

You should also take an overall look at the roof from outside the building. Is there any evidence of slipped tiles, or any obvious signs of moss or mould? Check around the perimeter of the roof at the sections which overhang (the fascias and soffits), and assess whether they in good condition. These are often made of wood, plastic or non-corrosive metal.

(example of slipped tiles, requiring attention)

(example of a soffit and fascia in good condition)

Are there any flat roofs? If so, you should check how old the roof is and - if you can - take a look at the top to see if there are any deformities. Any depressions in a flat roof will cause puddles in the winter, and could ultimately cause water ingress. Also, always bear in mind that flat roofs have a much shorter life span than pitched roofs. A normal and well-fitted bitumen flat roof (usually identified by seeing sheets of felt containing small stones) in most climates will usually have a lifespan of around 15-20 years, whereas a fibreglass flat roof (usually identified by having a painted look) is about double that lifespan.

(puddles on a flat roof can cause problems)

Outside

Whilst you're outside, there are a few other items which you can check.

If the area around the house is not flat, you should check for any visible signs of landslip or subsidence in the immediate vicinity of the building.

Are there any trees growing close to the house? If this is the case, this could affect the foundations of the building, particularly if the building is not built on pole foundations. If you're unsure about this, you should always seek advice from a structural engineer or a building specialist.

(example of tree roots potentially causing structural issues)

And check the drains and gutters - are they in good condition, and will they clear the water sufficiently? Pay particular attention to any drains immediately outside the home, because persistent soil dampness can also cause the foundations of the building to be compromised.

(example of insufficient drainage which, if persistent, could cause structural issues)

Other

There are a few other general items to also consider before making an offer:

- What fixtures and fittings are included?
- Are the included fixtures and fittings in a good state of repair?
- Is there double glazing?

Check any fitted cupboards, do they work correctly? Do the drawers open and close smoothly? What about the doors on the fitted wardrobes? Do they stick?

(example of a broken cupboard door, make sure they all work as expected)

For apartments or any other buildings with communal areas, always take the time to have a good walk around. Are there any obvious defects? Are there any plans to rectify issues and, if so, would there be a charge for residents?

(example of a communal area in bad condition, make sure you check this)

Conclusion

I think it is fair to say that you'll never find a property to be absolutely perfect and free of issues. But finding these issues as early as possible in the process will help you in making an informed decision as to whether you buy or not.

Of course you can appoint a building surveyor or other valuation specialist, but these services are not free. You should always have an idea of what you're getting yourself into before you make that offer to buy!

Hopefully, with the insights in this guide, you will be in a much better position to identify faults and to use these in your initial negotiation with the seller. Or indeed, find some defects which could be far too expensive to resolve, meaning that you can walk away from making an offer without spending any of your hard earned cash!

Remember, most of the challenges which are faced in any newly purchased home are those problems which arise unexpectedly. This is why it's very important to know what you're looking at, and to do your research.

On the next two pages is a basic checklist of the key items covered in this guide to help you with your next real estate viewing.

Good luck!

HOME VIEWING CHECKLIST

Structure	
Any wall cracks? Cement gaps between bricks or stones?	
Are walls & chimney straight, and not leaning or bulged?	
Damp	
Any peeling wallpaper? Yellow or brown staining?	
Any condensation on windows?	
Any black mould (most common in bathrooms)?	
Moss or algae growth on external walls?	
Rot	
Window & door frames – is the wood soft or crumbly?	
Door steps – is the wood soft or crumbly?	
Window sills – is the wood soft or crumbly?	
Skirting boards (base boards) – is the wood soft or crumbly?	
Original wood floors – is the wood soft or crumbly?	
Are the floors bouncy or firm? (wood floor joists)	
Security	
Burglar alarm – fitted & functional?	
Fire alarm, smoke detectors – fitted & functional?	
Security lights – fitted & functional?	
Is there a video doorbell?	
Door & window locks – are they adequate?	

Utilities	
Boiler type and last service date?	
Hot water tank and last service date?	
Age of electricity components? Last safety check?	
Gas appliances, last safety check?	
Condition of radiators & thermostats?	
Check control pipes for underfloor heating?	
Air conditioning unit age and last safety check?	
Do the water taps work, and the water drains quickly?	
Check the toilets flush?	
Roof	
Is attic insulated? Can any water stains be seen?	
Are there any slipped tiles?	
Around and underneath roof outside – in good condition?	
Flat roof condition?	
Outside	
Signs of landslip or subsidence nearby?	
Any trees near the house?	
Drain and gutters – will they clear water sufficiently?	
Other	
Which fixtures and fittings are included in the sale?	
Are the windows double-glazed?	
Do all fitted cupboards operate as expected?	
Defects to any communal areas?